BIONIC BODIES

HIGH-TECH BODY SCIENCE

MEGAN KOPP

REX

CRABTREE
Publishing Company
www.crabtreebooks.com

Author: Megan Kopp

Editors: Sarah Eason, John Andrews, and Petrice Custance

Proofreader and indexer: Wendy Scavuzzo

Editorial director: Kathy Middleton

Design: Paul Myerscough, Paul Oakey, and Jane McKenna

Cover design: Paul Myerscough

Photo research: Rachel Blount

**Production coordinator and
  Prepress technician:** Margaret Amy Salter

Print coordinator: Margaret Amy Salter

Consultant: David Hawksett

Produced for Crabtree Publishing Company by Calcium Creative.

Photo Credits:

t=Top, tr=Top Right, tl=Top Left, tc=Top Center, b=Bottom,
br=Bottom Right, bl=Bottom Left, bc=Bottom Center, r=Right,
c=Center, cr=Center Right

Aethon: 23r; Ekso Bionics: 10; ©2017 Intuitive Surgical, Inc. Used with
permission: 21r; Limbitless Solutions: 3DHope.com: 3, 15; Rex Bionics:
16br; Second Sight: 17tr; Shutterstock: 17c, Belushi 17cr, Willyam
Bradberry 4–5, ChooChin 17br, Ericsmandes 6–7, ESB Professional
29tc, Fusebulb 12–13, Elsa Hoffmann 8c, Ktsdesign 18–19, Jacob Lund
26–27, Master Video 20–21, Ahmet Misirligul 8–9, Monstar Studio 29tr,
Morphart Creation 28bc, Nerthuz 12, Olivier Le Queinec 26b, Denis
Ronin 14, Iaremenko Sergii 29br, Tinxi 5t, Wavebreakmedia 24–25; suitX:
11; Courtesy of syncardia.com: 16cr, 29bc; Shutterstock: Sportpoint front
cover; Wikimedia Commons: Jon Bodsworth 28bl, Dick Thomas Johnson
23l, Science Museum London 28t, Tabercil 17tl, Jiuguang Wang 22.

Cover: Shutterstock: By sportpoint

Library and Archives Canada Cataloguing in Publication

Kopp, Megan, author
          Bionic bodies / Megan Kopp.

(Techno planet)
Includes index.
Issued in print and electronic formats.
ISBN 978-0-7787-3584-7 (hardcover).--
ISBN 978-0-7787-3608-0 (softcover).--
ISBN 978-1-4271-1989-6 (HTML)

          1. Biomedical engineering--Juvenile literature. 2. Medical
technology--Juvenile literature. 3. Medical innovations--Juvenile
literature. 4. Robotics in medicine--Juvenile literature. 5. Bionics--Juvenile
literature. I. Title.

R856.2.K67 2017   j610.28   C2017-903591-6
                                                              C2017-903592-4

Library of Congress Cataloging-in-Publication Data

Names: Kopp, Megan, author.
Title: Bionic bodies / Megan Kopp.
Description: New York, NY : Crabtree Publishing Company, 2017. |
  Series: Techno planet | Includes index.
Identifiers: LCCN 2017027456 (print) | LCCN 2017031542 (ebook) |
  ISBN 9781427119896 (Electronic HTML) |
  ISBN 9780778735847 (reinforced library binding : alk. paper) |
  ISBN 9780778736080 (pbk. : alk. paper)
Subjects: LCSH: Bionics--Juvenile literature.
Classification: LCC Q320.5 (ebook) | LCC Q320.5 .K67 2017 (print) |
  DDC 617.9--dc23
LC record available at https://lccn.loc.gov/2017027456

Crabtree Publishing Company

www.crabtreebooks.com   1-800-387-7650

Printed in Canada/092017/PB20170719

Published in Canada
Crabtree Publishing
616 Welland Ave.
St. Catharines, Ontario
L2M 5V6

Published in the United States
Crabtree Publishing
PMB 59051
350 Fifth Avenue, 59th Floor
New York, New York 10118

Published in the United Kingdom
Crabtree Publishing
Maritime House
Basin Road North, Hove
BN41 1WR

Published in Australia
Crabtree Publishing
3 Charles Street
Coburg North
VIC, 3058

CONTENTS

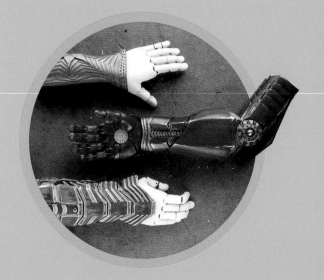

AMAZING NEW BODIES

The human body is amazing. It functions like a computer, with our brain sending messages to different body parts, allowing us to move and speak. However, just like a computer, things can go wrong with the human body. A part, such as an arm or heart, can become damaged or weak. That's where scientists step in. New technologies have made it possible to repair and rebuild the human body, and even make it stronger than it was before.

BETTER THAN BEFORE

In the 1970s, a television show called *The Six Million Dollar Man* was a smash hit. In the show, astronaut Steve Austin was badly injured when his experimental aircraft crashed. His body was rebuilt with mechanical parts that gave him superhuman powers. Many comic books, movies, and television shows have created characters like Steve Austin who develop extraordinary abilities through the use of technology. These stories have always been science fiction or imaginary tales of future scientific possibilities. However, something called **bionics** is quickly turning science fiction into reality.

Technology is pushing the start button for bionic body solutions.

UNDERSTANDING BIONICS

Bionics is a science that uses technology to create new working parts for living things. "Bio" means *life*. The ending, "onics," comes from *electronics*. The term "bionics" was first used in 1958—the same year the first **pacemaker** was put inside a human patient.

However, most of today's bionic bodies are not superhuman like Steve Austin's. Bionics simply allows people who need help to live better lives. Bionics can help a child who has lost an arm play catch, or a person who has gone blind to see shapes again.

The science of bionics includes advances in almost all parts of the human body, both inside and out. Bionic body parts can replace everything from arms and legs to eyes and ears to hearts and knee joints. The way bionic body parts look and work is becoming more and more lifelike. The world of bionics is changing all the time, with constant advancements in technology, such as robotics. Bionic bodies are no longer science fiction. They are here and now.

Iron Man is a comic book hero. He may not be real, but the technology behind him is quickly becoming a reality.

ARTIFICIAL ARMS AND LEGS

Leonardo da Vinci was a man ahead of his time. He was an artist, architect, engineer, and dreamer who lived 500 years ago. He drew sketches for inventions that would not actually exist for hundreds of years, such as the parachute, armored tank, and even a robot. Da Vinci also drew a sketch of an artificial leg. Today, many of da Vinci's dreams have become reality, including artificial limbs, which have improved countless lives worldwide.

WHAT IS A PROSTHETIC LIMB?

A **prosthesis** is an artificial body part designed to replace a missing body part. This could be a hand, arm, leg, eye, or ear. French surgeon Ambroise Paré created artificial hands and arms for wounded soldiers in the late sixteenth century. These were made of wood, metal, and leather. Until recently, artificial arms and legs were body-powered, requiring body movements to control the prosthetic limb.

New prosthetic legs are stronger and lighter.

JUST LIKE THE REAL THING

Making prosthetic limbs today is a mixture of art and science. Lightweight plastics and strong lightweight metals such as **titanium** are molded to look and feel like real hands and feet. Underneath the "skin," new electronic technology makes the limbs work like the real thing as well.

Myoelectric limbs use **sensors** placed in the body to send signals to an electric motor. The motor then moves the limb. The "power knee," for example, is a motorized bionic knee that copies muscle power. It provides lifting power for stairs and gently puts on the brakes for downhill slopes.

Making a hand move is more difficult. The i-limb is a prosthesis created by Touch Bionics. It slips over the damaged part of an arm. Small **electrodes** make contact with the skin and pick up electrical signals from the arm muscles. The signals are sent to a small computer, which tells the robotic hand to move. Tiny motors in the thumb and each finger allow the artificial hand to grip like a real hand.

TECHNO PLANET

In the United States, the Defense Advanced Research Projects Agency (DARPA) is working on a robotic arm that can be moved by thought control. A tiny device implanted inside a person's brain sends signals to the arm, telling it to move. This prosthetic limb could also bring back the sense of touch by sending signals from the arm to the brain.

BIONIC EARS AND EYES

People who have no problem hearing and seeing the world around them may not realize the challenges faced by people who cannot hear or see. In the bionic world, exciting advances are helping to change the lives of many hearing- and vision-impaired people.

CAN YOU HEAR COCHLEAR?

A **cochlear implant** is an electronic implant that replaces the function of a damaged cochlea, or inner ear. Hearing aids only make sound louder. Cochlear implants let hearing-impaired people detect sounds when hearing aids do not work.

A **processor** behind the ear picks up sounds and sends them to the implant inside a person's head. The implant turns the sounds into electrical **impulses**. These travel to electrodes inside the cochlea, which then sends nerve impulses to the brain, where they are translated into recognizable sounds. Researchers at the Massachusetts Institute of Technology (MIT) are working on a new, low-power wireless implant that does not need any outside parts.

SEEING CLEARLY

Some eye diseases destroy the cells in the back of the eye that pick up light. Placing a **microchip** in the eye can help some blind people detect patterns of light and dark, so they can see the outlines of objects. A camera mounted

More than 200,000 people around the world have received cochlear implants.

on a pair of glasses captures an image. The image is sent to the microchip as electrical signals. These signals are sent through the **optic nerve** to the brain. The brain figures out the information and allows the person to "see."

A United States company called Aira makes smart glasses for blind and vision-impaired people. The glasses feed images from the user to an operator sitting at a computer. The operator can see what is in front of the user and verbally guide him or her around city streets or through any other obstacles.

New technology is also underway to replace the eye's natural lens with a bionic lens. This new lens could make a person's eyesight three times better, close up as well as far away. It would be like having both a small magnifying glass and a pair of binoculars in your eyes!

Computer-controlled headsets that produce artificial but realistic sights and sounds may one day be a bionic reality.

LEVEL 5
CLEARANCE AUTHORIZATION

9

GEARING UP

We have skeletons inside our bodies. They help us stay upright and walk. Insects have skeletons on the outside of their bodies. They are called exoskeletons. The fictional character Iron Man wears a suit like an exoskeleton. And now, real life is not far behind. At the 2014 soccer World Cup in Brazil, a man paralyzed from the waist down made the first kick of the tournament using a robotic exoskeleton.

ROBOT ADVANCES

Several different companies have created exoskeletons. The EksoG, made by Ekso Bionics, is an exoskeleton with motorized legs. It helps people paralyzed in their lower body walk again, with the help of crutches. The EksoG has a powerful motorized frame and an onboard computer. The skeleton is strapped over the user's clothes. It has four motors that make it move. A battery pack is carried on the back.

The latest version is the EksoGT. It provides different levels of help, depending on a user's needs. As a person's strength improves, the exoskeleton gives less support. The wearer gradually uses more of their own muscle power. The EksoGT has been used in more than 130 **rehabilitation** facilities around the world.

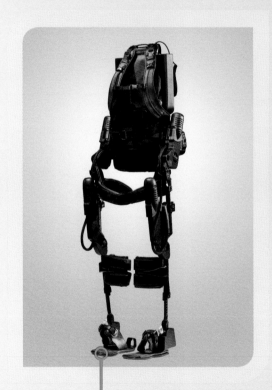

The EksoGT skeleton helps people stand up and walk sooner in their recovery process.

The lightweight Phoenix exoskeleton allows the wearer to walk at speeds up to 1.1 miles per hour (1.8 kph).

Bionic Power, a Canadian company based in Vancouver, has created PowerWalk, an exoskeleton worn on the legs. These bionic legs collect and store power from the movement of walking. This means soldiers may no longer have to carry heavy 20-pound (9-kg) batteries on their backs. Carrying less will help them move faster. The U.S. Army is testing this technology.

The Phoenix exoskeleton allows wearers to walk by pushing buttons in a pair of crutches. The buttons send commands wirelessly to the exoskeleton. The exoskeleton weighs about 27 pounds (12 kg) and costs around $40,000. A similar exoskeleton, called ReWalk, costs $70,000 and weighs about 50 pounds (23 kg). The ReWalk has a faster walking speed than the Phoenix. It moves at just over 1.6 miles per hour (2.6 kph).

INSIDE REPAIRS

Replacing body parts on the outside of the body with bionic parts is challenging. But try going inside! Our bodies have a natural defense system. If something foreign appears in our body, our immune system kicks into high gear and tries to get rid of it. This is a major challenge for bionic technology.

NEW FOR OLD

The **pancreas** is an organ in the body. It makes **insulin**, which keeps blood sugar levels down. A professor in England is working on an artificial pancreas. It has a **reservoir** of insulin surrounded by a gel barrier. When blood sugar levels rise, the excess blood sugar in the body's tissues soaks into the gel. This makes the gel soften, and insulin is released. When the blood sugar level drops, the gel hardens, and the insulin stops being released. The insulin reservoir can be refilled from a hole in the skin. It is a great idea. However, the immune system may reject the bionic pancreas.

In 2011, a cancer survivor in Sweden received the world's first artificial windpipe. Although the windpipe was artificial, it was coated with the patient's own cells to minimize rejection by the body. Artificial lung machines were developed in the 1960s. They work outside of the body as a temporary step to help patients who are waiting for lung transplants. Dr. Robert Bartlett and his staff at the University of Michigan are working on a totally artificial lung made of plastic that can be put inside the chest.

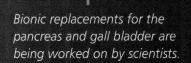

Bionic replacements for the pancreas and gall bladder are being worked on by scientists.

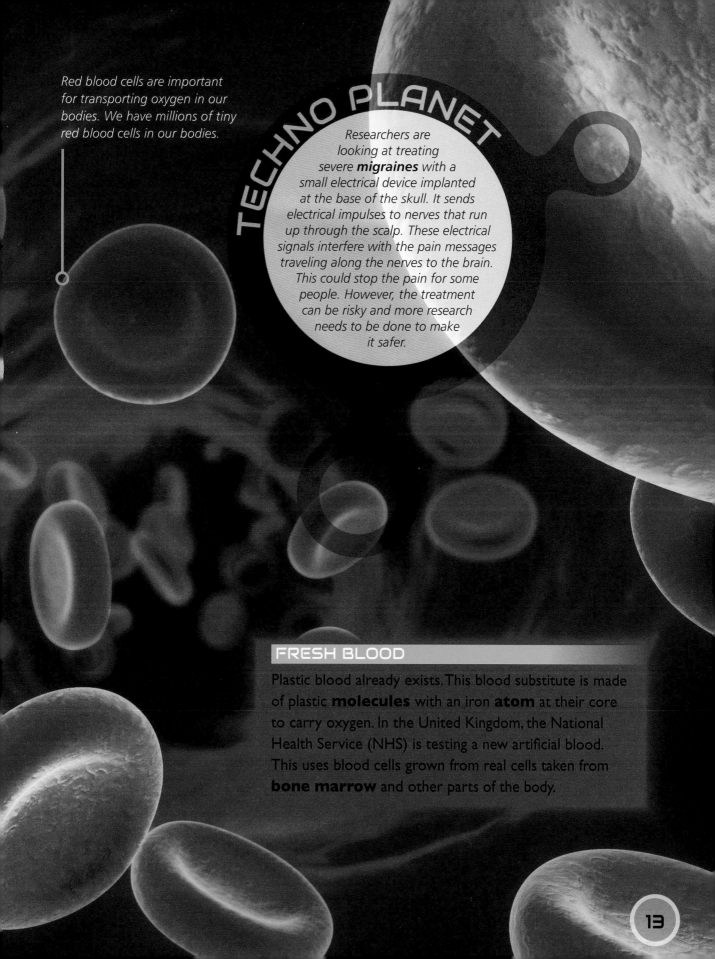

Red blood cells are important for transporting oxygen in our bodies. We have millions of tiny red blood cells in our bodies.

TECHNO PLANET

Researchers are looking at treating severe **migraines** with a small electrical device implanted at the base of the skull. It sends electrical impulses to nerves that run up through the scalp. These electrical signals interfere with the pain messages traveling along the nerves to the brain. This could stop the pain for some people. However, the treatment can be risky and more research needs to be done to make it safer.

FRESH BLOOD

Plastic blood already exists. This blood substitute is made of plastic **molecules** with an iron **atom** at their core to carry oxygen. In the United Kingdom, the National Health Service (NHS) is testing a new artificial blood. This uses blood cells grown from real cells taken from **bone marrow** and other parts of the body.

3-D BODY

Need a new ear? Print it out. Scientists and researchers can now make copies of body parts using three-dimensional (3-D) printers. This printer technology uses tiny pieces of plastic to create objects. It is similar to the way inkjet printers create pictures on paper by adding layers of ink. In this case, the computer software tells the printer to lay down layers of plastic in a pattern.

GOOD AS NEW

Scientists are using 3-D printing to create body parts. Sections of bone and muscle have been 3-D printed. They all work like the real thing when implanted into test subjects. In 2014, doctors in the Netherlands successfully replaced most of a woman's damaged skull with a 3-D plastic copy.

Going one step further, Japanese heart specialist Professor Makoto Nakamura has developed a 3-D bioprinter. It took three years to complete. The bioprinter can make humanlike tissue by adding layers of living cells rather than plastic. It can print a living tube that is similar to blood vessels, which are the tubes that carry blood around the body. Professor Nakamura hopes that one day even a heart could be bioprinted.

In the future, it may be possible to create a heart by using a 3-D printer.

PRINTED ARMS

Albert Manero is a mechanical engineer who leads a company called Limbitless Solutions. He saw the need for low-cost but fully working bionic arms for children. Manero, along with many engineering students and volunteers, set out to make 3-D-printed bionic limbs for children at no cost to their families. In 2015, they created the world's first 3-D-printed bionic arm for seven-year-old Alex Pring. Hollywood actor Robert Downey Jr. plays Tony Stark in the *Iron Man* movie series. He helped present Alex with his first bright-red, Iron Man-style, 3-D robotic arm.

Alex's cool new arm allows him the freedom to ride a bike like any other child.

FRANKLY BIONIC

Could you create a complete body from bionic parts? A group of engineers and scientists from the Smithsonian's National Air and Space Museum in Washington, D.C., did just that for a documentary film about bionics. The television program showed how much of the human body could be replaced by **circuits**, plastic, and metal. The result was a modern-day Frankenstein.

WALK THE TALK

To start, a bionic man would need to have a brain. A remote-controlled computer with specially designed hardware should work. Add in a "chatbot" computer program that turns text into speech. This allows the bionic man to carry on a simple conversation. Put the brain in a 3-D printed skull and attach a plastic face to keep everything in place. Use a pair of Argus II glasses for sight. Add a cochlear implant for hearing. Connect the mouth to the artificial lungs with a 3-D printed windpipe.

Artificial heart

In the same cavity as the lungs, place an artificial pancreas, kidney, and spleen. These **prototypes** exist, although they have a long way to go before they can be used in humans. Researchers have yet to create reasonable prototypes of an artificial stomach and intestines. No problem for a bionic man. Humans may get energy from food through digestion, but a machine gets its energy from external power sources.

Add a complete **circulatory system**. Use the same type of artificial heart that some patients use while they wait for a donor human heart. Pour in some plastic blood to flow through plastic veins. Attach prosthetic arms, hips, legs, knees, and ankles. Set the bionic body in a REX exoskeleton to allow the bionic man to sit, stand, walk, and turn.

REX exoskeleton

TOO CLOSE FOR COMFORT?

The result is a machine with more than two-thirds of the function of a human body. This brings up questions. Will robots replace humans in the near future? Some people think that this type of technology should be kept to a minimum. Others think that there are real benefits. What do you think?

Bionic glasses

Cochlear implant

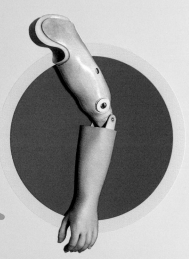

Prosthetic arm

Bionic parts made from plastic, metal, and electronic wiring can carry out many, but not all, of the body's functions.

Bionic ankle

NANOBOTS

In the 1966 movie *Fantastic Voyage*, a medical team was shrunk down to **microscopic** size to enter a scientist's body and save his life. Science fiction, right? Of course, people can't shrink down that small. However, scientists are working on tiny medical devices that can travel through our blood vessels. **Nanotechnology** in medicine is not science fiction. It is science fact.

HOW SMALL IS NANO?

"Nano" comes from the Greek word for *dwarf*. Nanotechnology is technology on a teeny-tiny scale. One nanometer is one-billionth of a meter. Look at a page in this book. It is about 100,000 nanometers thick! Medical researchers are using nanotechnology to create nano-sized robots, or nanobots. Canadian researchers from Montreal have developed nanobots to fight cancer. These smaller-than-tiny robots act as nanotransporters. Their cargo is a load of **chemotherapy** drugs. The nanobots are programmed to take their shipment along the most direct path to reach deep inside a **tumor**. They deliver the drugs to the exact spot where they will be the most effective in fighting the cancer.

DOOR-TO-DOOR CURE DELIVERY

Drug delivery may one day be as simple as mind over matter. Scientists are working on drug nanobots with special locks. The locked nanobot travels to where it is needed in the body. The lock opens when the mind says to open. The drug is then released. When brain activity stops, the lock closes again, and drug delivery stops. If this works, people will be able to trigger a drug when they need it just by thinking about it.

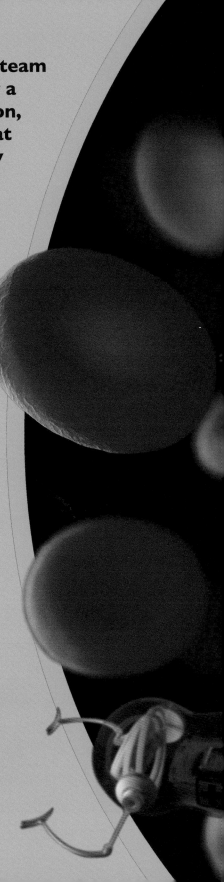

Nanobots need to be as tiny as red blood cells to travel through blood vessels around the body.

TECHNO PLANET

"Quantum" means a tiny amount of any form of energy, such as light. Quantum dots are tiny pieces of material that send out **infrared** light. Researchers hope to direct them to specific areas in the body, such as cancer cells. Doctors can spot the light that quantum dots give out. It lets them look deeper into the body than ever before.

DR. ROBOT

The artist Leonardo da Vinci drew see-through pictures of the human body. In honor of his role in the history of medicine, a surgical robot has been named the da Vinci machine. This human-operated robot makes delicate and precise surgery possible.

The machine has microscopic vision. It has tiny instruments that can bend and rotate better than the human hand. The doctors can see better and have more control. Surgeons operate through just a few small incisions, or cuts. They control the robotic system at all times. By 2020, sales of surgical robotics are expected to almost double to $6.4 billion.

SMART TOOLS

Imagine a surgical knife so smart that it knows whether the tissue it cuts is cancerous or not. No need to imagine. The intelligent knife, or iKnife, does just that. Developed in London, United Kingdom, the iKnife takes old technology to a whole new level.

Electricity is used to heat tissue during surgery to minimize blood loss while a surgeon makes incisions. The iKnife analyzes the smoke that is produced. It detects what chemicals are there. The chemicals reveal information about the condition of the tissue. In these operations, surgeons want to take out as little healthy tissue as possible but still make sure all of the cancer is removed. The iKnife is more than 90 percent accurate.

Stethoscopes and doctors go hand in hand. Doctors use stethoscopes to listen to sounds in the chest. Smart stethoscopes update this familiar tool. The new devices either attach to a regular stethoscope, or are separate with a set of headphones. They take the chest sounds and send them wirelessly to a computer or smartphone. The doctor sees the sound waves instead of just hearing them. The devices allow doctors to share recordings with other medical professionals and even store data in the patient's electronic health record.

The da Vinci machine allows for delicate and precise surgery.

Robot-guided operations are no longer a futuristic idea. They are becoming more routine.

CAREBOTS

If you have been in a hospital or medical facility, you will know that they are busy places. Healthcare workers carry out many different tasks. Sometimes one task has to wait because another is more important. Enter carebots! Carebots are robots that support and help healthcare workers. They can take over simple jobs that need to be repeated again and again. Carebots work 24 hours a day, seven days a week, without needing to take time off due to family emergencies or illness.

HEALTHCARE HELPERS

Infections during hospital stays can lead to death. Keeping hospitals free of dirt and germs is difficult. The Xenex Robot is a cleaner. It uses **ultraviolet** light to disinfect spaces in healthcare facilities quickly and efficiently.

Heavy lifting? There is a robot for that. TUG can carry more than 1,000 pounds (454 kg) of medication, laboratory specimens, or other sensitive materials. Robear is a bear-shaped robot that can lift patients out of bed and into a wheelchair. It can also help patients stand, or turn patients in their hospital beds to avoid sores.

Blood tests are routine during many hospital stays. Veebot is a robot that draws blood. It does the job in less than a minute and correctly chooses the best vein to use more than 80 percent of the time.

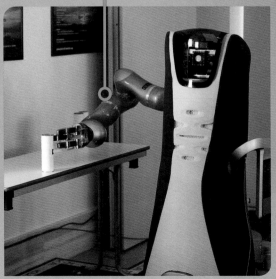

This Care-O-bot robot can help patients by picking up objects that they cannot reach or hold.

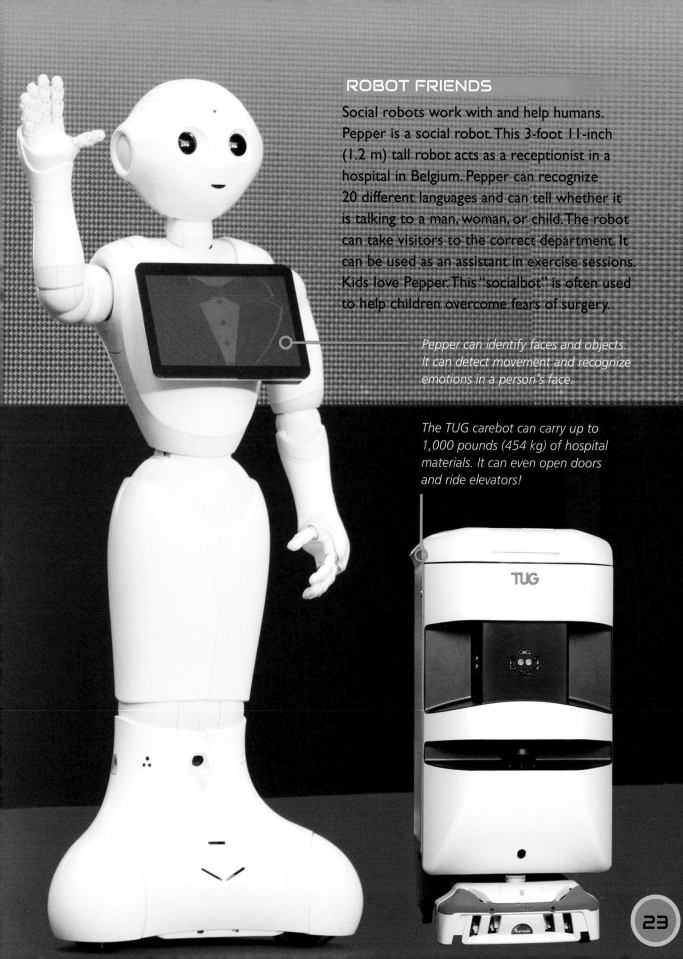

ROBOT FRIENDS

Social robots work with and help humans. Pepper is a social robot. This 3-foot 11-inch (1.2 m) tall robot acts as a receptionist in a hospital in Belgium. Pepper can recognize 20 different languages and can tell whether it is talking to a man, woman, or child. The robot can take visitors to the correct department. It can be used as an assistant in exercise sessions. Kids love Pepper. This "socialbot" is often used to help children overcome fears of surgery.

Pepper can identify faces and objects. It can detect movement and recognize emotions in a person's face.

The TUG carebot can carry up to 1,000 pounds (454 kg) of hospital materials. It can even open doors and ride elevators!

TUG

TECHNO TESTING

Collecting information about how the body is working is an important part of healthcare. But what if the thought of a blood test makes you feel faint? Google may have the answer. It has filed a **patent** for a needle-free, blood-testing smartwatch.

PAIN-FREE MONITORING

Google's smartwatch could make life easier for **diabetics**. These people have to regularly monitor their blood sugar levels. To do this, they prick a finger for a small sample of blood. The smartwatch instead fires microscopic material painlessly into the skin. A droplet of blood is then sucked back into the watch for testing. Google also has a patent on smart contact lenses that use the fluids in a patient's eye to monitor blood sugar levels.

24-7 TRACKING

Wearable testing kits can sense, record, and send information all day, every day. Think bionic Band-Aid. These patches are made up of a flexible electronic material that is comfortable and durable. Some bionic Band-Aids can track temperature. The patch monitors the patient's temperature and sends the information to a smartphone or computer.

A smart microchip can monitor different chemical levels inside the body. It is less than ½ inch (1.3 cm) long. The microchip is implanted under the skin and wirelessly sends information to a patient's doctor via a smartphone. However, the microchip only lasts for about six weeks. Scientists are working on ways to expand its lifespan.

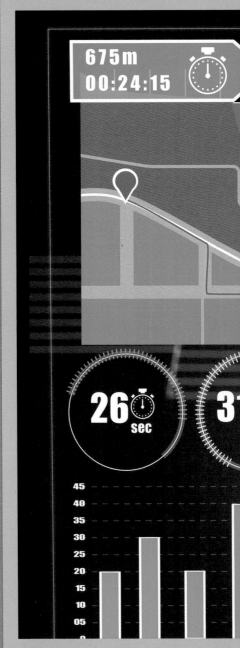

Monitoring body systems has become a high-tech business.

Other health-monitoring patches can be worn like a tattoo. These patches do not need batteries. The stretchy skin patch uses light pulses to monitor such things as heart rate and the amount of oxygen in the blood. Radio signals from a nearby phone or tablet power the device and let it send information.

+1.0%

-.54%

-0.3%

+6.7%

+2.6%

cel

261 step

63 BPM

TECHNO PLANET

The QardioCore is a wearable heart monitor with no patches or wires. It uses sensors to measure heart rate, breathing rate, and skin temperature. It also tracks activity. All this information can be read on a smartphone and shared with medical professionals.

FUTURE FANTASTIC

What does the future hold for bionic bodies? There is a lot of visionary thinking happening, and technology is constantly improving and advancing. However, turning visions into reality may be a whole different story.

WHOLE BODY REPLACEMENT

A surgeon from Italy thinks it may soon be possible to **graft** a living person's head onto a donor body. He hopes that body transplants could be used for people affected by terminal diseases. This doctor thinks the technology is nearly there. However, other surgeons and scientists disagree. They believe full body transplants are far into the future.

FROZEN FOR THE FUTURE

Cryogenics is the science that looks at how very low temperatures happen and how they affect other things. Cryogenics has many uses. It can fast freeze some biological materials such as human blood and tissue. The freezing of parts of the body to destroy unwanted or bad tissue is known as cryosurgery. It is used to treat cancers and abnormalities of the skin, cervix, uterus, prostate gland, and liver.

Test tubes containing such things as human blood or tissues are frozen in cryogenic containers.

Freezing an entire human body after death in the hope of later restoring life is known as **cryonics**. There are three cryonic facilities in the United States and one in Russia. Does it work? Not yet. People who believe in this practice hope that future scientists will figure out how to bring the bodies back to life.

SHELVING YOUR BRAIN

Cryonic facilities also offer the option of preserving just the head. The idea is that in the future it could be attached to a new body. If that sounds too far-fetched, how about digital brain preservation? Regular cryonics tries to preserve the biological features of a person's body or brain. Digital brain preservation involves uploading our minds to a computer, so we live on in a digital form. In the future, the digital brain could be woken up and uploaded into a computer simulation or robotic body.

Preserving human heads with cryonics is not yet a reality. Who knows what the future will bring?

TECH TIMELINE

300 B.C.E.
Wood and bronze artificial right leg from a man in Capua, Italy, found in 1910

early 1500s
Mechanical iron hand with moving parts built for the knight Gottfried von Berlichingen

1945
United States National Academy of Sciences founded the Artificial Limb Program

1997
German company Ottobock designed C-Leg with built-in microchips to control knee joint movement

700 B.C.E.
Artificial wood and leather big toe found on an Egyptian mummy in 2000

500–600
Artificial left foot on man in Austria, found in 2013

1912
D.W. Dorrance patents the split-hook prosthetic hand after losing a limb himself

1960s
Russian researchers develop myoelectric prostheses activated by nerve impulses

2004
*A **quadriplegic** becomes first patient for brain-computer interface technology*

2008
Japanese researcher Makoto Nakamura pioneers bioprint technology

2013
Canadian company Spring Loaded Technology introduces Levitation, the first bionic knee brace

2014
Woman in Brazil receives first 3-D-printed skull replacement

1998
Professor Kevin Warwick tests chip implant technology on himself

2006
Artificial bladders first "grown" from patients' own body cells

2008
First fully functional artificial heart developed

2014
Researchers in Switzerland grow a replacement nose

2016
U.S. Food and Drug Administration approves the world's first artificial pancreas

GLOSSARY

Please note: Some **bold-faced** words are defined where they appear in the book.

atom The smallest part of a substance

bone marrow The soft tissue inside bones

chemotherapy The use of chemicals to treat disease, especially cancer

circuits The complete pathways of electric currents

circulatory system The system that moves blood around the body

cochlear implant An electronic device that does the work of damaged parts of the inner ear (cochlea)

diabetics People with the diabetes disease, whose bodies cannot control the amount of sugar in their blood

electrodes Points where electricity flows into or out of something

foreign Unrecognized by an immune system

graft Join new tissue to existing tissue

immune system The system that protects the body from harmful things

impulses Waves of energy that can pass through the body

infrared Invisible light beyond the red end of the color spectrum

insulin A hormone that regulates the level of sugar in the blood

microchip A group of electronic circuits on a tiny piece of material

microscopic Extremely small

migraines Throbbing headaches that can affect vision and make people feel sick

molecules The smallest parts of a substance that still have all its features

myoelectric Powered through a muscle's natural electric impulses

nanotechnology The science of engineering practical, but very small, things

optic nerve The nerve that sends signals from the eye to the brain and allows us to see

pacemaker A small electrical machine put inside a person to make the heart beat evenly

paralyzed Unable to move part of your body

patent A legal document giving the inventor of an item sole rights to build or sell it

processor A device that picks up and sends information

prototypes Early versions of something

quadriplegic A person who cannot move their arms or legs

rehabilitation Bringing back to normal

reservoir A holding area for liquids

sensors Devices that can be placed in a body to send information

stethoscopes Medical instruments used to listen to a person's heart or lungs

three-dimensional (3-D) A shape having the three dimensions of length, width, and height

tumor A lump or mass of cells in the body that is not normal

ultraviolet Invisible light beyond the violet end of the color spectrum

visionary Looking beyond the ordinary

LEARNING MORE

BOOKS

Bethea, Nikole Brooks. *Discover Bionics (Searchlight Books: What's Cool About Science?)*. Lerner Publications, 2016.

Mercer, Bobby. *The Robot Book: Build & Control 20 Electric Gizmos, Moving Machines, and Hacked Toys*. Chicago Review Press, 2014.

Parker, Steve. *Super Human Encyclopedia*. DK Publishing, 2014.

Wilson, Daniel H. *Popular Mechanics Robots: A New Age of Bionics, Drones & Artificial Intelligence*. Hearst Books, 2015.

WEBSITES

http://limbitless-solutions.org
See how Limbitless Solutions are creating personalized 3-D printed bionic limbs and other solutions for disabilities.

www.explainthatstuff.com/prosthetic-artificial-limbs.html
Find information on topics related to science and technology on the Explain That Stuff! website.

www.livescience.com/12954-bionic-humans-artificial-limbs-technologies.html
The Live Science website looks at the top 10 bionic technologies that are being used on humans.

www.smithsonianchannel.com/shows/the-incredible-bionic-man/0/3378516
Watch videos about Frank, the bionic man, on the Smithsonian Channel.

INDEX

About the Author

Megan Kopp is the author of more than 75 books for young readers. She wishes she had a bionic brain that could store all of the nuggets of knowledge she uncovers during research.